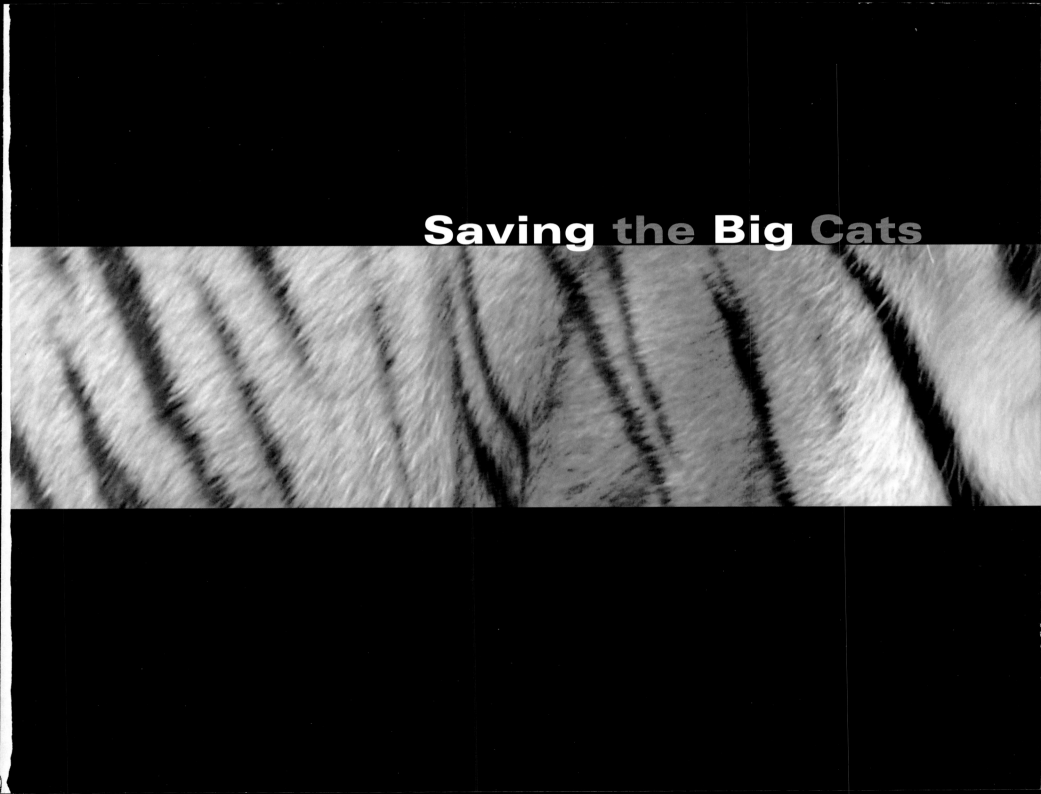

Saving the Big Cats

QUARRY BOOKS

an imprint of

INDIANA UNIVERSITY PRESS

Bloomington & Indianapolis

Stephen D. McCloud

Saving the Big Cats

The Exotic Feline Rescue Center

This book is a publication of

Quarry Books

an imprint of

Indiana University Press

601 North Morton Street

Bloomington, IN 47404-3797 USA

http://iupress.indiana.edu

Telephone orders   800-842-6796

Fax orders   812-855-7931

Orders by e-mail   iuporder@indiana.edu

Manufactured in China

Library of Congress Cataloging-in-Publication Data

McCloud, Stephen D., date
  Saving the big cats : the Exotic Feline Rescue Center / Stephen D. McCloud.
    p. cm.
  ISBN 0-253-34609-6 (cloth : alk. paper)
  1. Felidae—Indiana—Center Point. 2. Felidae—Indiana—Center Point—Pictorial works.
  3. Exotic Feline Rescue Center (Center Point, Ind.) 4. Wildlife rescue—Indiana—Center Point.
  I. Title.
  QL737.C23M329 2005
  639.97'975'0977244—dc22

                                                    2004028193

  1 2 3 4 5 11 10 09 08 07 06

There are two means of refuge from
the miseries of life: music and cats.
—Albert Schweitzer

The smallest feline is a masterpiece.
—Leonardo da Vinci

Contents

Leo, a.k.a. Hiss

Foreword

Cats have a long association with people, a relationship for which the small, domestic cat is best known. Bones and mummified remains of the domestic cat, descended over 4,000 years ago from the African desert cat of Egypt, have been found among the possessions of the pharaohs. Surprising to many, however, is the similarly ancient relationship of the much larger cheetah. Ornaments depicting cheetahs with collars around their necks, dated between 700 and 300 B.C., have been found in burial mounds in the Caucasus. In 1474 one Armenian ruler owned 100 hunting cheetahs; following the acquisition of his first cheetah, named Fatenbaz, Akbar the Great of India developed a collection that reportedly numbered over 9,000 cats during his lifetime. But that was then and this is now.

For thirty years I worked at a public, medium-sized zoo. And for thirty years, I was offered an animal a day by the public. *Each week* one of those offerings was a large carnivore, usually a large felid. Most of these generous offerings were lions, tigers, or pumas; all were turned down. I am supposed to be retired now but am still called upon to help county sheriffs and humane society officials in this state and others deal with a tiger or lion in a backyard or shopping mall. Some things never change: just a few weeks ago, when two tiger cubs were found abandoned in rural North Carolina, I and a number of other zoo professionals were contacted to provide ideas about where these animals could be placed—for the next twenty years. The worst scenarios I face always involve tigers, and in every case, the animals' owners claim they were involved in tiger conservation and that they were going to "domesticate" this animal. Where does this foolishness come from? All these cats are of untraceable origin and none have any link to tiger conservation. Neither are they domesticated, or even tamed, nor will they ever be. In many cases, law enforcement officials have no other option than to humanely destroy the animals, an onerous job at best.

This scenario is acted out each week by zoos, sanctuaries, and rescue centers in state after state because some people just don't get it. In a recent meeting of the American Zoo and Aquarium (AZA) Tiger Species Survival Program (SSP), the AZA Tiger SSP asked each attendee to identify the three most significant issues facing tiger management in this country. Without hesitation, the group felt that the number one problem was not disease, diet, or captive breeding but rather the exploding private ownership of tigers: this includes keeping tigers as pets, the rapidly expanding number of tigers being offered for sale to unqualified members of the public, canned hunts, and so forth. While the group made no value judgment on private owners, it did generate a separate opinion that reflects the professional opinion of the AZA Tiger SSP management group. Had this group been the AZA management group for lions, leopards, jaguars, or pumas, not to mention bears, wolves, and poisonous snakes, the outcome would have been the same. Zoo professionals have come to realize one simple fact—big cats make bad pets. Period. In the case of the AZA management groups for large cats, it is their unanimous opinion that they do not endorse the private ownership of large cats in non-AZA locations.

How is this proliferation of private ownership possible? The sad reality is that in many areas of the United States, it is still legal for private individuals to possess large species of cats, that is, tigers, lions, jaguars, leopards, and pumas, often obtaining them from other private breeders and animal dealers who sell them as "pets." The management groups of the various AZA felid programs believe that potential buyers should be but rarely are made aware of the problems associated with ownership of large felids. After years of experience answering phone calls from private individuals offering a "pet" tiger that is no longer manageable, helping local humane and wildlife officials track down escaped pumas, and assisting lawmakers to craft laws that will reduce the scope of private ownership in state after state, animal professionals oppose the keeping of large felids as pets for very sound and widely repeated reasons.

Wild cats are inherently dangerous to the individuals who possess them, to their neighbors, and to the community at large. More than the domestic dog, cats are obligate carnivores. In layman terms, this means that they can only exist on a diet of meat and to do this, cats have developed predatory instincts that over tens of millions of years have evolved to the point that cats are among the most consummate predators. Most importantly, captive-born wild cats of all sizes retain these wild instincts for life. They are all prone to sudden and unpredictable episodes of aggressive behavior, and are capable of inflicting serious and even fatal injury to humans. Worse yet, the instinctual, often lethal, predatory behavior in felids is frequently directed toward children. Those owners who mistakenly think they can domesticate a large cat, or even tame one, should get a dictionary out and look up the word "domesticate." In fact, domestication takes hundreds, often thousands, of years of careful selection, allowing humans time to weed out individuals possessing bad habits, such as aggression. The last species of animal to be domesticated was the rabbit—by farmers in France—an action officially recognized by the Catholic Church during the 1500s. Any individual

that thinks they can domesticate a puma or a tiger in a year or two is truly out of touch with reality.

Risks associated with attacks by large cats on people in the wild are well documented. In the case of tigers, perhaps the biggest feline offender within the private sector, the number of specimens maintained in captivity far exceeds the number in the wild, but relatively little is known about risk of injury or death associated with owning and managing captive tigers and other large carnivores. To bring the danger posed by private ownership of large cats into better focus, consider this: the Captive Wild Animal Protection Coalition reported that the rate of human injury and death from big cats has reached an all-time high—in 2003, there were at least 33 incidents involving captive big cats. Of these incidents, 3 were human fatalities and another 14 involved human injuries; hundreds more cats either escaped or were confiscated. These statistics include the near fatal attack on Las Vegas entertainer Roy Horn, the rescue of a tiger from a Harlem apartment, and the discovery of dozens of dead tigers in California. In 2004 there were at least 7 incidents involving big cats, resulting in 1 human death, 2 human injuries, and 4 big cat escapes. Of these animals, 6 had to be shot. Also 5 more were found dead, and at least 10 seized. In the United States, from 1998 to 2001, tigers alone injured 27 humans and killed at least 7, a rate equaling 1.75 fatal attacks per year. And this does not include the additional 6-plus non-fatal attacks per year. All but one fatal attack in the U.S. occurred where tigers were privately owned or in private facilities. Forty-two percent of victims were classified as

visitors and almost one-quarter of victims were under the age of 20. In a separate study from 1998 to 2001, an analysis of 30 international media sources and additional documents uncovered 59 unique incidents where people were reportedly injured or killed by captive tigers. What does this mean? Without question the most common denominator visible in these results suggests that victims typically underestimated the dangers posed by direct contact, not to mention personal ownership, of these animals.

Owning a large cat is costly and time consuming. Among other things, appropriate housing requires considerable space and its design must accommodate the cat's physical and psychological needs. Moreover, this doesn't begin to address security measures adequate for preventing escapes and injurious interactions with humans and domestic animals. In some states, enclosures must be double fenced, warning signs posted, and should a cat escape and cause injury or death to people or livestock, the owner may be charged with a felony.

Exotic felid ownership is a long-term, twenty-four-hour commitment of twenty years or more. Providing the proper housing, nutrition, and veterinary care is extremely expensive and difficult, and much more than the average person can provide. Large felids acquired when they are young and more manageable lose their appeal as they grow in size and unpredictability. These then become the animals that end up in sanctuaries, often arriving in poor health because the owners lacked the knowledge or financial ability to adequately feed their charges. When owners decide to dispose of their animals and find that zoos and sanctuaries are full, many of these animals are euthanized, abandoned, or doomed to live in deplorable conditions. Many exotic cats must be euthanized if homes—qualfied zoos or sanctuaries—cannot be located, and especially if they bite someone (State Board of Health regulations), in order to be tested for rabies.

In stark contrast to the carefully nurtured populations of large cats maintained in American Zoo and Aquarium Association zoos, most of the wild felids in private hands lack traceable pedigrees, are probably severely inbred, and have essentially no "conservation value." Kept as pets and isolated from managed populations, these animals and their owners contribute nothing to scientifically developed conservation programs designed to maintain genetic viability and insure the survival of their species. Most owners do not realize this aspect of private ownership until they try to "dump" one on the nearest zoo or roadside menagerie. AZA zoos are not in the position to take in these orphaned felids, usually of unknown origin, because the space they have is limited and structured for managed conservation programs. The only thing that can be said of this situation is that the private ownership of large cats does not involve the taking of cubs from the wild because nearly all large felids are regulated by the U.S. Endangered Species Act and thus not available for importation from the wild by the pet trade. Rather, they are being bred in the backyards of states with lax exotic animal laws and thereafter sold widely across the country, often to individuals in states where possession is illegal.

Zoos at the local and national (AZA) level are trying to help local, state, and national authorities develop ways of resolving the problem of private ownership, including the illegal or ill-conceived acquisition of exotic animals as well as ways of handling the resulting donations once they do occur. All this is being done in addition to educating the public about the inadvisability of large felids as pets. AZA felid management groups believe that AZA zoos can be increasingly effective in curbing the pet trade's selling of large felids to the public by working with their local governments. Targeted actions include eliminating the sale, trade, or other disposition of large felids by zoos to animal dealers known to be active in the pet trade. The underground "zoo" can be stopped only if states make it unsafe for these individuals to do business. Many zoos are recruiting the participation of their educators in the development, production, and distribution of materials advising the public of the problems inherent in ownership of large felids, disseminating that material to the market areas of potential owners targeted by the pet trade. If this level of education starts early, some young, impressionable potential buyers may get the message before doing something they and an exotic cat will regret later.

Zoos and AZA groups are helping state agencies to investigate existing state regulations to form an overview of the extent and effectiveness of current legislation, often using Florida's regulations as a model. By supporting local and state authorities in the enforcement of current legislation, and supporting legislative bodies in their proposals and enactment of improved legislative restrictions appropriate to effectively prohibit the selling of large felids by the pet trade, more and more states are essentially becoming big cat–free. AZA groups also help legislative bodies contradict claims by those who support private ownership of tigers and other large felids that risks associated with owning and showing these animals is insignificant. Rather, zoo professionals conclude that the growing number of people owning tigers and other large exotic animals is cause for concern because of the danger to the animals, to handlers, and to the public. The problem of private ownership of dangerous exotic animals has broad implications for tiger and large carnivore conservation, public health, and animal welfare, and zoos support the regulation of private ownership of dangerous exotic animals and encourage scientific analysis of this contentious issue.

The international trade in exotic animals that includes the U.S. is estimated to be a billion-dollar industry, second only to illegal drugs. The 2004 USDA list of licensed and registered exhibitors totals more than 2,000 facilities, an increase of 20 percent over the last five years. Three federal laws regulate exotic felids—the Endangered Species Act, the Public Health Service Act, and the Lacey Act. These laws primarily regulate the importation and interstate commerce of exotic animals; unfortunately they often have little impact on the private possession of large cats. In 2005 President Bush signed into law the "Captive Wildlife Safety Act" (H.R. 1006, S. 269) that was supported by the AZA and many animal protection organizations. The bill prohibits anyone from importing, exporting, transporting, selling, receiving, acquiring, or purchasing in interstate commerce prohibited wildlife. This bill was deemed necessary because only thirteen states regulate privately held exotic animals (Ark., Calif., Colo., Ga., Hawaii, Mass., N.H., N.Mex., N.J., Tenn., Utah, Vt., Wyo.), banning private possession of exotic animals (i.e., they prohibit possession of at least large cats, wolves, bears, monkeys, and dangerous reptiles). Another seven states (Conn., Fla., Ill., Md., Mich., Nebr., Va.) have a partial ban (i.e., they prohibit possession of certain exotic animals but not all). More (15) states (Ariz., Del., Ind., Maine, Miss., Mont., N.Y., N.Dak., Okla., Ore., Pa., R.I., S.C., S.Dak., Tex.) only require a license or permit to possess an exotic animal, a situation that leads to all too frequent national headlines when a large cat injures or kills someone, or a large collection of felids is found dead or dying in a private collection. As for the remaining states, many neither prohibit possession nor require a license, or at best only require some information from the possessor (veterinarian certificate, certification that the animal was legally acquired, etc.).

Where are we going with this? I like to think that states are slowly getting the message, and that more people who might have seriously considered obtaining a large cat are having second thoughts about it. Indeed, I think most states understand the dangers. The same probably cannot be said about today's potential buyers, but if states get tough, there will be few exotic animals available to buy. I hope so.

Alan H. Shoemaker
Columbia, S.C.

Preface

I FIRST VISITED THE Exotic Feline Rescue Center in Center Point, Indiana, on September 1, 2001. An acquaintance of mine, Michelle Hall of Bloomington, Indiana, had repeatedly suggested that I visit the place and contribute whatever I could. Her enthusiasm finally got to me, and one Saturday morning I left Terre Haute, Indiana, for Center Point, in search of lions and tigers. After half an hour of searching, I finally found the Exotic Feline Rescue Center (EFRC), two miles south of Center Point on a gravel road.

I paid $10 and was told to "have a good time." Everyone was busy; no one said, "Stay three feet back from the fence" or "Tigers like to spray." No one offered to take me on a tour. Visitors are required to have a worker with them at all times, but I seemed to have slipped through the cracks. And no one asked me about the $6,000 worth of digital camera equipment I was carrying. I had expected a small zoo, but what I found was indescribable. There is no zoo in Center Point.

I returned the next day, and Joe Taft, the founder of the Center, remembered seeing me the previous day. He cast suspicious looks my way as he stopped on his bicycle to chat. "You must have enjoyed yourself yesterday," said Joe. "You have a very dangerous place here," I think I replied.

After visiting zoos for more than forty years, I found EFRC to be a breath of fresh air. There was no concrete—which felines do not like—and there was nothing non-essential to the well-being of the animals. EFRC was more of a real home for the cats.

As I was on my way out that first day, Jean Herr-berg, the assistant director of EFRC, noticed the camera and said, "If you get any good pictures, we would like to see them." I just smiled. I knew I'd be back many times.

The images in this book were taken over almost three years, with four different digital cameras and numerous lenses. The famous Nikon 80-200 AFS produced at least 95 percent of the images. I replaced it with the even more incredible Nikon 70-200 AFS VR in 2004. The stories were taken from EFRC newsletters and from interviews with Joe and Jean. My personal comments came from spending hundreds of hours with the felines, something I recommend to everyone—not just "cat people."

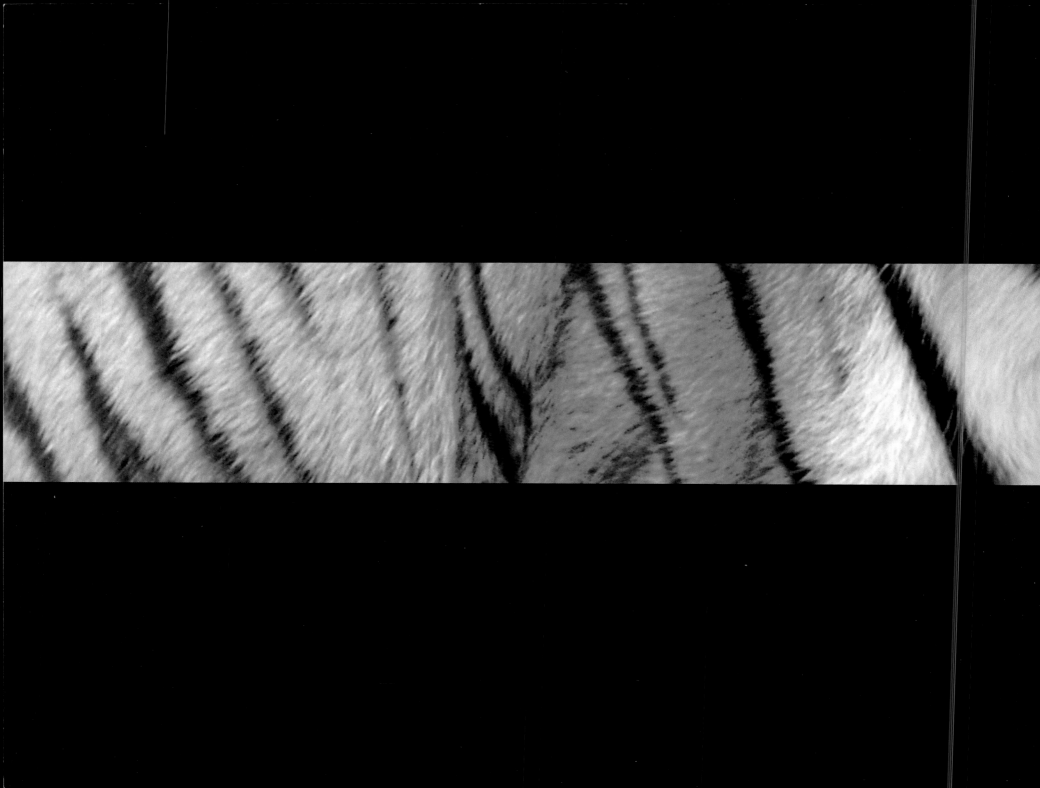

Clyde, October 2004

The Origins of **EFRC**

JOE TAFT was twenty years old when he walked into a pet shop in Terre Haute, Indiana, and bought an ocelot. Although today Joe strongly disapproves of exotic pet ownership, his fantasy at the time was to drive around fast in a Lotus with a cheetah in the seat beside him. He settled for an MG and an ocelot.

After college, Joe moved onto six acres in New Mexico, where he acquired a one-year-old female leopard. Taaka, as he named her, lived with him as a house pet. She had a large outdoor area and the run of the house for nearly nineteen years. Shortly after Taaka's death, Joe bought a thirteen-day-old leopard he named Kiki.

When Kiki was about six months old, Joe happened across a couple of badly abused tigers, BC and Molly. This was his first experience with the mistreatment of exotic felines, and he was outraged. He rescued the two cats—and thus began the effort behind the Exotic Feline Rescue Center.

In 1991, Joe left New Mexico and returned to Indiana with Kiki, Molly, and BC. He looked for a piece of land where he would have no immediate neighbors. The fifteen acres he purchased are now the developed portion of EFRC. The nonprofit corporation that was subsequently formed to support the Center purchased another eleven acres. Someone later donated money to purchase eighty-two additional acres on the south side of the road. This area has not been developed; it serves as a buffer between EFRC and the outside

world. Kiki, Molly, and BC stil live at the Center in their original cage.

"If you build it, they will come"—and come they did. Soon someone called and asked whether Joe could take a lion. Then someone else called, hoping that he could take another unwanted feline. Suddenly there were five lions. Then a cougar. Then a bobcat. Then many, many more. All were taken in on a permanent basis. When a big cat finds its way to the Exotic Feline Rescue Center, it has a home for life.

One of the most frequently asked questions by new visitors to EFRC is, "Where do all these animals come from?" The usual answer is circuses, zoos, breeders, and people who had them as pets. Sometimes the animals arrive singly. At

other times they come by the truckload. That was the case in the summer of 2000, when the Center added a large group of exotic felines from one of the worst facilities ever discovered. On August 21 of that year, EFRC workers traveled to Pittsburgh, Pennsylvania, intending to return with two or three lions, which they hoped to introduce to a group of young lions already living at the Center. When they arrived at the facility, they found neglect and abuse beyond belief. In a dark basement that reeked of feline urine and feces were four cages about five feet by five feet. There were three lions in one cage, three tigers in a second cage, and one tiger each in the other two cages. Seven of the cats were severely malnourished and dehydrated; they apparently had been left there to die. They weighed 50 to 80 pounds instead of the 200 to 250 pounds that a healthy lion or tiger their age should weigh. The eighth was closer to normal size but still substantially underweight. Fearing that none of these felines would survive, EFRC workers loaded all of them into a truck and headed for Indiana. It was the first time in a long time that the animals had seen sunlight or breathed fresh air.

Two weeks later, a semi pulled up at EFRC. In it were eight more lions and tigers that had been seized by the USDA from the same person in Pennsylvania. After years of citations for violations of the Animal Welfare Act, fines in 1997 and 1998 totaling $32,000, and revocation of the owner's license, this facility had finally been closed.

Another tiger that had been rescued in Pennsylvania by the USDA was initially placed at a rescue center in Mississippi. He became extremely aggressive there, injuring his cage mate and human staff, so on September 9 he too was transferred to EFRC. He settled in nicely and has become a favorite of most of the workers. Maybe it's the name Felix, or maybe it's because of his friendly behavior; he never has an unkind word for anyone. He loves his new life and seems to have completely forgotten the abuse he suffered in the past.

Joe and Jabberscat, April 2002

Jean feeding a baby tiger, February 2003

There are many other "rescue centers." Few, however, come up to the standards of EFRC, and EFRC is probably the largest in the United States. Some visitors come expecting to see a zoo. When was the last time you saw a blind tiger at a zoo? Or a lynx with neurological problems? Or a puma with frostbitten ears? Zoos want, and more importantly keep, only "perfect" animals. Whereas zoos are concerned with species survival, EFRC is concerned with individual survival.

When EFRC was incorporated in 1996, there were only about 20 animals housed at the facility, and all the work was done by volunteers. Twelve years later, there are 166 exotic felines at the Center, and a nine-member board of directors oversees an annual budget of more than $160,000. Joe now has full-time employees to help with the animals' upkeep, but the Center's volunteers still play an essential role. They contribute in many ways: in addition to preparing food and feeding the cats, they clean cages, paint signs, give tours, and write stories for the newsletter.

Jean Herrberg is the assistant director of EFRC. Sometime in the mid-1990s, she started coming to the Center as a volunteer. She arrived just in time to hand-raise two baby lions, Spirit and Parker. After traveling back and forth to her teaching job in Columbus, Indiana, Jean decided to retire from teaching and move to Center Point—her original home, where she still had family. Jean spends much of her time traveling around the country picking up animals, doing educational programs, producing the newsletter, answering mail, and feeding the animals.

After one lion died during minor surgery at the office of a local veterinarian, the EFRC staff started taking animals to the University of Illinois—a two-hundred-mile round trip. In 2004, a new building was erected at the Center with space for an operating room. With various donations of operating room equipment, surgeries can now be performed on the grounds.

When Joe Taft rescued BC and Molly all those years ago, little did he know where his act of kindness would lead. With the help of dedicated staff and volunteers and the generosity of donors who share Joe's passion for these big cats, the Exotic Feline Rescue Center has been able to expand its mission: to give these special animals a dignified life in a permanent home with the best of care. The photographs in this book are a testament to the resounding success of that mission.

Monica, October 2003

the Big Cats

ACHIA

ACHIA arrived at EFRC in April 1998. A one-year-old puma, she had been living with a family without the proper permits and was confiscated by Animal Control in Champaign, Illinois. It was determined that she had been fully declawed and was being fed cat food. Achia is extremely friendly and is one of the most beautiful animals at EFRC. She has been featured on a t-shirt and note cards. Until sufficient donations can provide her with a larger living area, however, she remains difficult to see on the standard EFRC tour.

Achia, October 2002

8

BC, MOLLY, & KIKI

BC (Blind Cat) is a 450-pound tiger that was born on July 3, 1990. He and his partner, Molly, had been used in a photography business, and they had been living in the back of a Volkswagen van while their owner traveled around the country. When they grew too large to be useful for that purpose, the photographer decided to get rid of them. Their health needs had never been addressed, and when they came to live at the Center, six-month-old BC was already crippled and blinded by cataracts, and most of his baby teeth had rotted. His sight has since been restored through surgery, and his strength and mobility have greatly improved through proper diet and exercise. He shares his enclosure, which includes part of the old house, with Molly and a female leopard named Kiki.

Two tigers living with a leopard is a strange sight. They are all affectionate with each other, but Kiki appears to be the feline in charge. Molly seems to have a hatred of photographers and just about anyone else whose name is not Joe.

Kiki, June 2002   *Kiki, September 2002*

Kiki and Molly, July 2002

10

Kiki, October 2003

Ben, September 2002

BEN & MONICA

BEN, a male puma, and MONICA and Lilly (Granny), female pumas, were among a group of animals that were seized from an illegal breeding operation in Illinois. They were the only three to survive. Today the pumas live in a 7,000-square-foot enclosure with lots of trees and brush in which to hide and play. They all enjoy visitors.

Monica with Ben behind her, January 2003

BOBBETTE

BOBBETTE, a female bobcat, is the most dangerous feline at EFRC. It isn't her fault. She's small, she's cute, she purrs, and you just want to hug her—but like all bobcats, she's solid muscle, and she can remove flesh in an instant. (Why do people want to keep these animals as pets? They can turn on you in an instant. It's the way nature made them.) Most people are wise enough to stay back from Bobbette's cage.

Bobbette was badly abused. Housed in a small cage for years, she continued to pace in a figure-eight pattern after moving into larger quarters. She seems to have overcome this behavior for the most part. Despite her dangerous demeanor, she's a favorite with most of the workers. If you're at EFRC when there's a lot of vegetation and you can't find Bobbette, walk quietly and slowly around her cage. You will almost certainly hear her growl or purr.

Bobbette, March 2002

14

Bobbie Sue, August 2003

BOBBIE SUE

BOBBIE SUE, a female tiger, came to EFRC from a man in north-central Indiana. The facilities for his animals were nice, but because he was in failing health, he could no longer keep them. They included Maggie, a female lion who lived with Coco for a long time, and a male lion named Ty who grew up with Bobbie Sue.

After Ty died, Bobbie Sue lived alone in a large cage with three shelters. Raja Boy, a male tiger, was placed in with her, but they kept attacking each other. Another male tiger, Jafar, was placed in with her, but she kept attacking him. Apparently she didn't want to share her mansion.

Bobbie Sue died in 2003, of unknown causes. She is dearly missed. With her curled-up tail and her great personality, she was very popular with workers; she always came up to the fence to visit. Four young tigers now occupy her large cage.

BOOMER

BOOMER, a male puma, arrived at EFRC in 1999 with a female puma named Donner. Born in Montana, they were captured there by a Fish and Game officer after their mother was killed by a hunter. The officer's plan was to release them back into the wild, but when that proved unworkable, EFRC sent two people to Montana to pick them up. At the Center they were eventually moved into a secluded 6,000-square-foot enclosure with a climbing tower. In spite of their shyness, they quickly adapted to their new home, eating well and rapidly gaining weight.

Boomer and Donner are not on the standard EFRC tour and are seldom seen except in the winter, when the vegetation is gone. Even then they can be hard to find. Boomer is not as shy as his sister and seems to have developed an interest in photography.

Boomer, July 2004

BRUMBY

BRUMBY, a black leopard, was born at EFRC. His mother was one of a group of badly neglected leopards that were brought to the Center after they were confiscated from a couple in California (see "The California Leopards"). She gave birth soon thereafter, and Brumby was the only cub to survive. He quickly became special to everyone— even after he helped destroy an expensive satellite receiver. Duct tape comes in handy with baby felines. Brumby now lives with Pauli Ann, a puma a month younger than he is. Their area includes a climbing tower, and Brumby spends a lot of his time at the top.

THE CALIFORNIA LEOPARDS

ON APRIL 22, 2003, California Fish and Game agents raided the home of a couple who were operating a so-called sanctuary. There they found thirty dead tigers and other big felines scattered around the property in various stages of decomposition; sixty-one dead cubs packed into freezers; thirteen tiger and leopard cubs in an attic, alive but dehydrated and near death; two alligators in a bathtub; and a young tiger tethered on the patio. The couple's eight-year-old son was living with rotting food, dead cubs, animal tranquilizers and hypodermic needles, mounds of trash, and animal feces in every room. Sixty-three charges were filed against the couple, including seventeen counts stemming from allegations of child endangerment and animal cruelty. On July 21 of that year, a judge issued the order to remove the animals.

Eight leopards from this facility arrived at EFRC on August 2 at 3:00 A.M. Six were unloaded and transferred to their new enclosure. Two were put into isolation—one because of his critical condition, and one because she looked as if she would deliver cubs at any moment. Every one of the felines was in horrible condition, but Bear, a large black leopard, was the worst. He was totally non-responsive, dehydrated, and near death. EFRC's veterinarian evaluated him and initiated immediate around-the-clock care. For several days he was given liters of IV fluids, administered without anesthesia—he was too weak to care.

Bear, August 2003

Bear, June 2004

18

Leopard from California, fall of 2003

Two weeks later, Bear had improved enough to be taken to the University of Illinois Veterinary School to get an evaluation of his general health and broken teeth. The doctors deemed it too risky to anesthetize him in his condition at the time, so he was brought home and nursed for three more weeks, then taken back for another evaluation. This time he was strong enough to be anesthetized, and several rotted and broken teeth were removed. Thereafter he made tremendous progress. He was later neutered by EFRC's veterinarian, Dr. Froderman. After an appropriate time, he was reunited with the seven females that had arrived with him. They were not as ill, but they were all underweight, one had a deformed spine, and most had dental problems. Three arrived pregnant, but only one cub survived (see "Brumby").

The leopards now have an expanded area with a climbing tower. They are not on the tour and will probably remain in their secluded area. No one believes they will ever forget their past or get used to humans. One of the great fringe benefits of working at EFRC is getting to visit with them.

Leopards from California, fall of 2003
(right and facing page)

Leopards from California, June 2004

CHARLIE

CHARLIE's glowing eyes are a reminder of what years of neglect can do to an innocent feline. The twelve-year-old puma was rescued by a couple who found him in a home in Jennings County, Indiana, sleeping in a rusted metal barrel, with grass growing in his water because of all the mud at the bottom. Charlie's face was scarred, and he was terrified of people. His owner was not even aware that he was blind. Charlie was in such poor health that when he was taken to the University of Illinois Veterinary School, they felt that they could not anesthetize him for a complete evaluation without undue risk to his life. They did say that nothing could be done to correct his sight, that he had damage to his throat from a choke chain, and that he had severe nutritional deficiencies. Since his arrival at EFRC, Charlie has gained weight and developed play behavior. He enjoys the company of the regular staff and volunteers.

Charlie, July 2002

CHICA & SINBAD

Two workers from EFRC traveled to south Texas to pick up Chica, a female bobcat, and Sinbad, a black leopard, along with a male tiger named Cain. They were among twenty felines whose owner had died. The location was well off the beaten track, and no one is certain if these cats were pets or were being used for something else. In any case, the man had made no plans for what was to happen to the animals upon his death.

Unlike the other two bobcats at EFRC, Chica is calm around humans—she goes off and hides. She is difficult to find, even in winter. She can sometimes be seen on her climbing tower. She lives near Bobbette the bobcat, and tour guides usually give up trying to find Chica and merely point out that she and Bobbette are similar.

Sinbad, a black leopard, appears to have had it rough in his former life. He moves slowly because of a dislocated shoulder, but he loves playing with tree limbs. He is one of the first animals on the EFRC tour, and his enclosure is the point at which every tour guide says, "This is what people usually call a black panther. Black leopards are not black; they are brown with black spots." He has a curly tail, which on rare occasions he uncurls. He seems quite content at EFRC.

Chica, October 2002

Chica, February 2002

Sinbad, October 2001

Sinbad, October 2003

Zavata, August 2003

THE CIRCUS TIGERS

ON LABOR DAY in 1997, ten tigers gave their last performance at the Circus Hall of Fame in Peru, Indiana. Ranging in age from three to fourteen, the tigers had been badly abused throughout their years in captivity. Zavata, Kashka, Prince, Olaf, Princess, Bombay, Mauza, Moustafa, Menelik, and Goldie had spent most of their lives in small cages. Their move to the Exotic Feline Rescue

Center afforded them large areas with climbing towers and water pools—luxuries they had never experienced.

A few of the original five circus cages can be seen near the EFRC entrance. They come in handy sometimes in transferring animals from truck to cage, or in moving them to the on-site clinic.

Zavata, who was fourteen years old when she

Zavata, May 2004

Prince, April 2004

Menelik, April 2004

arrived at the Center, is the mother of most of the other circus tigers. The circus experience took its toll on Zavata. Her canines had been cut off, causing severe infections in many of her teeth. She was transported to the University of Illinois twice for root canals and recovered nicely. She had to be anesthetized for more than thirteen hours over the course of both procedures.

Kashka was also fourteen years old when she arrived at the Center. She is not related to Zavata. Her canines had deep grooves cut into them, and she required serious dental attention as well.

Prince and Olaf were born in 1989 to Zavata. Olaf lived with Kashka until his death in July 2004. Prince lives with Princess, and they are known for being very unfriendly to humans.

Bombay, Mauza, Moustafa, and Menelik were born in 1994 to Zavata. Menelik prefers her own cage and now lives contentedly by herself. She can frequently be seen using her climbing tower as a scratching post.

Big Boy and Tuffy were born to Princess at EFRC. Big Boy is aptly named. He is probably the largest tiger at EFRC, although Otis might take

exception to that statement. Big Boy and the other four circus tigers born at EFRC share a large enclosure with a climbing tower and water tank. They like to hide in the brush next to the fence and spray visitors. Suma, Tora, and Layla were born to Kashka at EFRC. Jean raised these five from babies, and they can get quite excited when she comes to feed them.

Tora, May 2004

Tuffy and Big Boy,
October 2002

CLYDE

CLYDE, a male lion, came with a female lion named Eula from a woman in Zionsville, Indiana—just outside Indianapolis. She was a breeder-dealer who took exceptionally good care of her animals. At one time you could see a herd of the woman's zebras as you entered Zionsville. She gave up Eula because Eula was a poorly adjusted animal—possibly because she had been fully declawed and had trouble walking. She gave up Clyde because Joe liked Clyde and wanted him. Clyde and Eula can sometimes be seen on the tour during winter. At other times they are well hidden by vegetation. Clyde always seems to look like he just got back from the barber shop.

Coco with Maggie in the background,
December 2002

COCO & MAGGIE

WHEN COCO arrived at EFRC in April 1995, he was not yet two years old, but his life had already been filled with pain and neglect. He was a hundred pounds underweight, and he understandably had a very bad attitude. He had been sold to a family in Marengo, Ohio, by a man who assured the family that the young lion loved children. Prior to that, Coco had suffered a broken leg and two fractured toes as a result of beatings with a baseball bat. Pins had to be inserted in his left hind leg so that he could walk. Coco's life at the Center was a happy time. The staff called him their "Rasta" lion because his mane resembled the dreadlocks worn by the Rastafari in Jamaica. Sadly, he died of renal failure in early 2004.

Maggie (originally Maggie Magoo), a female lion, came from the same man who had Bobbie Sue. Maggie was the first animal to be taken to the University of Illinois for surgery to correct her vision. She and Coco shared a large area. Maggie likes to flirt with the three big boys to the south and can really cause an uproar. Coco came to accept her evil ways and finally stopped chasing the boys away.

Coco, April 2003

CUBBIE & RAPPIE

CUBBIE, a male lion, came to EFRC in 1997. He was a little over two years old and had gotten too big for his owner to take care of. He had been kept in a town near EFRC in a small pen with a five-foot-high fence and no roof. It is amazing that he never escaped. If he had, he almost certainly would have been killed by authorities.

Rappie, a female lion, arrived in December 1996, when she was four to six months old. Found tied up in a woodshed, Rappie was underweight and malnourished, with severe facial lacerations. She had been seized by the authorities in Lima, Ohio, and taken to the local humane society. The society contacted EFRC after seeing the Center on the television show *Inside Edition*.

For several years Cubbie lived next to Koshka (a female tiger) and Rappie. When Koshka died in 2004, Rappie was moved in with Cubbie. They immediately took to each other, and Cubbie now spends a lot of his time defending her from visitors. He couldn't be happier.

Cubbie and Rappie, June 2004

Emmett, November 2001

EMMETT

EMMETT, a very young puma, was found by a small girl somewhere in eastern Illinois. He was running loose, dragging a leash behind him. "Mommy, can I keep him?" He was transported to EFRC by the Illinois Department of Natural Resources. His owner was never found. Upon arrival at the Center, the young feline was given the name Emmy. Shortly thereafter, it was discovered that he was an Emmett—which came as quite a surprise to the EFRC workers. Emmett and another EFRC puma now live at the Louisville Zoo, on permanent loan.

Gabby Girl, March 2004

GABBY II (GABBY GIRL)

GABBY GIRL's former owner was a man from Hennepin, Illinois, who had a large, expensive, all-solar house and kept three tigers, a puma, and Gabby Girl in expensive chain-link cages. He made the mistake of going in with two of the tigers. They attacked and killed him, and the police then had to kill the tigers in order to retrieve the man's body.

Gabby Girl, in contrast, may just be the friendliest female lion in the world. She lived behind the tool shed when she arrived at EFRC, and she could often be seen peeking around the top of the shed. She now lives in a large enclosure next to Cubbie and Rappie.

India, July 2004

INDIA

INDIA is a white tiger who most likely came from a white tiger breeder. She's small and dark, so she probably isn't very desirable as white tigers go, but she is a favorite with visitors. She was two and a half years old when she arrived at EFRC on September 28, 2001. India is very gentle, probably because she's blind—not uncommon among white tigers. She will lick your hand if you give her the chance. At one time she had a large swimming pool, but she never went near it—probably because of her blindness.

White tigers are controversial. Developed through inbreeding, they serve no conservation purpose and are bred for strictly financial reasons.

India, April 2004

India, October 2003

To produce white tigers or any other phenotypic curiosity, zoos and facilities must continuously in breed, father to daughter, to granddaughter, and so on. This is a contradiction of the fundamental genetic principles upon which all survival programs for endangered species in captivity are based. Most zoos have stopped breeding white tigers, but the tourists they attract are hard to give up.

Jabberscat & Lester

Jabberscat and Lester came from Las Vegas, but not together. The two male lions live with Kimba, a female lion from Dallas, Texas. Lester had been used in the photo business. Jabberscat came at the request of Joe. He had been living at the same place where Kiki, Joe's second leopard, was once boarded. Jabberscat was EFRC's first lion. Lester arrived shortly thereafter. One of the funniest things I have ever seen at EFRC was Jabberscat and Lester resting on a large piece of meat—not fighting, but neither one willing to give it up. These three are not on the tour, but they can be seen at a distance at the end of the tour.

Jabberscat and Lester, March 2004

Jagger, May 2003

JAGGER

JAGGER, a male tiger, was used in a photography business in Las Vegas until he killed his trainer. After that, he was apparently dragged around the country before being abandoned in Minnesota. When the woman who owned the property where he was left called EFRC and asked if they could take him, Jean drove out and picked him up.

It's just another one of your typical tiger-in-the-photo-business stories.

Joejoe

Joejoe, a male puma, was originally named Joe Puma. He was illegally held and inadequately housed at his former home next to an elementary school, from which he had escaped twice. His former owner seems to have—well, there's a lot more to the story, but perhaps it doesn't need to be put in print. Joe will probably tell you all about it if you ask. Joejoe does not seem to like workers or visitors, but he does seem to enjoy his large enclosure. Tour guides usually try to point him out because he is cross-eyed.

Joejoe, July 2002

King, July 2004

KING, JASMINE, & LAUREN

On July 22, 2001, King, a fourteen-month-old African lion, came very close to death. Housed in a small kennel in Minnesota, in a barn surrounded by horses, dogs, and a bear, he had been fully declawed and had received very little attention or exercise. His owner, having decided that she could no longer afford to feed him, was planning to have her brother shoot him and take him to a taxidermist if another home could not be found for him that day. Lucky for all of us, King was saved by a woman named Wendy, who borrowed a horse trailer for temporary housing until she could find

King, September 2001

him an experienced, legal, and qualified permanent home.

After hearing about King, the Center agreed to take him. Wendy delivered him to Indiana—a fourteen-hour drive. When EFRC workers unloaded King later that day, they found him to be an extremely friendly lion in need of a good diet and lots of attention.

Within a few days of taking in King, EFRC found out about Jasmine, a female lion at a movie ranch in Idaho who also needed a home. Since a new enclosure was being constructed for King, the Center decided to take Jasmine, too, hoping that they would like each other and become companions. The two were housed next to each other to get acquainted. Within days they were moved into their permanent home, which includes numerous trees and a climbing tower.

No one realized that King was old enough to breed. The result was Lauren, who now lives with King and Jasmine. Jasmine made good use of the climbing tower when Lauren got to be too much to deal with. King required that anyone wanting to see baby Lauren first give him lots of attention. The King enclosure is now one of the most popular at EFRC.

Jasmine, September 2003 (top), and April 2004 (bottom)

45

Lauren, June 2003 (above), and October 2003 (facing page)

LANKY

LANKY, a male lynx, came to the Center as part of a large rescue effort carried out by several facilities in June 2004. A man in Ohio had been in legal trouble for years because of his substandard treatment of exotic animals. (A tiger he owned had even mauled his two-year-old son to death.) After repeated problems over a long period of time, the USDA declared the facility to be "unclean and unsafe," and the man was soon ordered by a judge to remove his approximately sixty animals. In early June of 2004, trucks arrived to begin hauling them away.

The rescued animals included fifteen tigers, two leopards, one black leopard, eight lions, one puma, one lynx (Lanky), and one female Himalayan sun bear. Lanky and two leopards ended up at EFRC. Others ended up at sanctuaries in Colorado and North Carolina, and at the Western Pennsylvania National Wild Animal Orphanage south of Pittsburgh. Nine black bears remained on the property while officials tried to find homes for them.

Lanky will soon move into his new area at the Center. He had dental problems when he arrived; those have been repaired, and he no longer appears to be in pain, but he does appear to have suffered some neurological damage at some point in the past. The two leopards that arrived with Lanky are living in separate temporary cages near the new building, and are slowly growing accustomed to their new home.

Lanky, July 2004

Leo, February 2002

LEO,
A.K.A. HISS

LEO, a beautiful male caracal, is commonly referred to as Hiss. The story goes that a woman in Michigan bought him as a baby for $3,000, unaware that he would get so big and would urinate in her house. Leo ended up at the Detroit Humane Society, and they called EFRC. He is not on the tour because he is easily stressed—as is anyone who gets near him. He is declawed but not deteethed.

Leo, July 2002

Majae, November 2002

MAJAE

MAJAE, a female serval, arrived at EFRC in early June of 2002. She had been found on a porch in Bloomington, Indiana, being fed cat food, and had been picked up by the local humane society. The Bloomington facility did not feel qualified to house an exotic feline, so they asked EFRC to take Majae. The owner was finally found, but he no longer wanted her. She had escaped from every owner she had ever had.

Majae is one of three servals, two female and one male, at EFRC. They all exhibit the same behavior—they want nothing to do with humans

Majae, June 2003

Majae, November 2002

Majae, November 2003

(or each other, for that matter). Attempts to introduce a male serval to Majae were unsuccessful. She spends most of the day in her shelter but occasionally ventures out. She shows considerable interest in a wild house cat that stops near her cage to eat. Although servals are supposed to be water animals, Majae showed no interest in a small pond in her cage, and it was eventually removed.

The Munchkins, October 2002

THE MUNCHKINS

IN THE SUMMER OF 2000, EFRC rescued five tigers and three lions from an unbelievably abusive situation at a facility in Pennsylvania. While all eight of them were severely underweight, the lions and four of the tigers were in particularly poor condition, suffering from malnutrition and dehydration. Because of their stunted growth, caused by the neglect they had suffered in their former life, the Center staff dubbed them "the Munchkins." Within a year, however, they had tripled in size. The smallest of the seven, a tiger named Isabella, went from 50 to more than 170 pounds.

Isabella suffered a broken leg while trying to play in partially frozen water in her swimming tank at EFRC, so a plate was placed in her left rear femur in mid-February 2001. She recovered nicely. If house cats have nine lives, then tigers must have at least a hundred.

Although they are extremely playful and were a highlight of the tour, the Munchkins have been moved to a much larger area off the standard tour. Because the four tigers are much more playful than the lions, this is an interesting group to watch.

The Munchkins, December 2002 (top), and February 2004 (bottom)

55

The Munchkins, April 2004 (above and facing page)

MURPHY

MURPHY, a male puma, was owned by some people in Chicago, Illinois. When they were caught with an illegal animal in the city, they took him to relatives in Gary, Indiana, where he soon escaped. He was confiscated by Gary city officials, and the owners never asked for him back. Gary officials called EFRC and quickly transported him to the Center in a police car. Murphy is quite playful and likes pretty much everyone—except, that is, for a certain photographer. He is not on the tour (unless he is on his climbing tower), but he can frequently be heard making friendly sounds.

59

NONA

NONA, a female tiger, was originally called No Name, but EFRC dubbed her Nona. Her mother was a pure white tiger at the Cincinnati Zoo. Nona came to EFRC through a man who has a big facility in Kansas where he buys and sells animals.

She was in a constant state of panic when she arrived at the Center, and it took her several months to adjust to her new home. She now lives there calmly and contentedly.

NYLA

ON JULY 21, 2000, the Capital Area Humane Society of Columbus, Ohio, contacted the Columbus Zoo asking for assistance with the confiscation of a young female tiger. Zoo staff met with the humane society officers at a warehouse only minutes from downtown. There they found Nyla, a well-adjusted, though underweight, tiger cub about four months old. When the owner of the cub could not be located, she was taken in by EFRC.

The owner of a nightclub had apparently purchased Nyla at an auction in the Midwest for several thousand dollars. He brought her back to the club to use in a promotion. The winner never claimed her, however, and for several weeks she remained confined to a crate in the back room of the club. The club owner then sold her to the man who had been in charge of the promotion, and that man soon gave her away. In four short months, little Nyla had changed hands at least four times.

When EFRC took Nyla in, they discovered that she had a cataract in her left eye, most likely due to poor nutrition. She underwent successful surgery to restore at least some vision in that eye. She also had developed an abscess from a broken right upper deciduous canine tooth, and the tooth had to be extracted.

Nyla now shares a large area at the Center with Cuddles, Jody, and a male tiger named Casey, who arrived on July 3, 2001, from New Mexico. Nyla is the most playful of the group and loves to interfere with picture taking.

Nyla (on left), May 2004

OTIS & BABY

OTIS, a very large male tiger, and Baby, a female lion, live in a large enclosure with an underground area and a goldfish pond. No, felines do not eat goldfish; they have a goldfish pond because Joe likes goldfish. Otis is officially named Otis Lee, but he is usually referred to as Odie. Whatever you

call him, he is definitely one of the largest tigers at EFRC. And he doesn't like cameras. He gets in the pond and waits for photographers who are too slow to avoid being splashed.

Baby came from the same woman in Zionsville, Indiana, who had Clyde and Eula. Odie came

Baby and Otis, March 2004

from a woman who was in financial trouble. Because Baby was living alone and was quite lonesome, and because she was the same age as Odie (both were very young), they were placed together. It was love at first sight. Neither has been neutered, but they have lived together for quite a while without incident. If Baby ever does give birth (not likely at this point), it will be her last. EFRC does not breed exotic felines. Baby can frequently be seen gossiping with Maggie, a female lion who lives next door.

Baby, April 2002

Parker, Tao, and Tucker, March 2002

PARKER, TAO, & TUCKER

PARKER, TAO, AND TUCKER are three male lions that share a large enclosure with an underground area near the visitors' entrance to EFRC. Parker's father, Clyde, is still at the Center, as is Lester, the father of Tao and Tucker. Tucker was the first cat born at EFRC. These three lions ignore visitors, for the most part, but they certainly don't ignore Maggie, their neighbor to the north. When they aren't flirting with her, they seem to work on coming up with new poses for photographers. They make a very impressive entrance to EFRC.

Parker, Tao, and Tucker, October 2002 (top), and September 2003 (bottom)

PAULI ANN

PAULI ANN, a very young female puma, was a surprise Christmas gift for a woman in Illinois. Not surprisingly, the woman couldn't take care of the little feline, so she and the gift giver contacted EFRC. Pauli Ann may have been obtained at an auction in Missouri, but she could have come from almost anywhere. Hard as it is to believe, exotic animals can be obtained from hundreds of individuals and at auctions and swap meets across the United States. Federal and state authorities do little to stop this kind of trade.

Pauli Ann now lives behind the new building along with Brumby, who is only a month older. Pauli Ann is the more playful of the two, but she is always able to persuade Brumby to join in. Brumby insists that the top of the climbing tower is his.

Pauli Ann, July 2004

Pescha, June 2002

Pescha, August 2004

PESCHA

PESCHA, a female puma, came to the Center from Nashville, Indiana. Left outside in a winter storm with no food or shelter, she was starving and her ears were frostbitten down to one-inch nubs when she was rescued by the same couple who took in Charlie, the blind puma that is also now at EFRC.

Pescha can be quite playful and seems nicely adjusted to her new home. The original spelling of her name was Peshia, but it somehow got changed when the sign was made for her enclosure. She has never expressed any objection to the new name.

RAJA BOY

RAJA BOY, a male tiger, was rescued along with the Munchkins from the basement of a house in Pennsylvania. Jean and some EFRC workers drove out there to pick up a couple of felines and came back with eight. Though Raja Boy was in somewhat better condition than the others, he was found to be suffering from a rotted tooth, which eventually had to be extracted. He was left with a slightly "goofball" look as a result, which fits his personality quite well. Workers have taken to calling him "Elvis." After Bobbie Sue's mate, Ty, died, they tried to introduce her to Raja Boy, but with no success. So Raja Boy now lives in his own area. His favorite activity is trying to attack photographers and spray visitors as they go past his enclosure.

Raja Boy, July 2003

Raja Boy, September 2003 (overleaf)

Lea, October 2002

RAKE, WEDGE, & LEA

RAKE, A MALE LION, AND WEDGE AND LEA, female lions, were born at EFRC on March 13, 1997. They are the offspring of Lester and Kimba. (Lester had a vasectomy soon thereafter!) After a few days with their mother, the cubs left the Center to be fostered by Jean. She had previously raised Spirit, Parker, Tao, and Koshka. Living with Jean and her house cats, the cubs became well socialized to humans. Because Jean was a fifth grade teacher in Columbus, Indiana, the cubs also went to school every morning. Weekends were spent at EFRC.

Within a few weeks, Rake and Wedge were able to assume their first real job as goodwill ambassadors for EFRC and as educators about the plight of exotic felines and other endangered species throughout the world. As Koshka and the other lion cubs did when they were young, Rake and

Rake, September 2002

Rake and Wedge, October 2003

Wedge traveled to several area schools, including Catlin Elementary in Catlin, Illinois, South Side Elementary in Champaign, Illinois, University Primary in Urbana, Illinois, and Park Ridge Elementary in Columbus, Indiana. The cubs helped teach schoolchildren about lion behavior and about wildlife conservation and environmental preservation. The children got to pet the cubs and raised more than $1,000 for the Center.

Lea was born with a deformed hind leg. As a result, she had a series of surgeries at the University of Illinois. According to Joe, she "practically lived there" for a while. She still moves with a limp, but she gets along fine.

At one time Cosmo, a male lion, lived with Rake and friends. In the first half of 2004, Cosmo got a new home in New Mexico. Cosmo and Rake had been fighting quite frequently, and when the opportunity to give Cosmo a happier home came up, Joe and a worker drove him to New Mexico so that Joe could see for himself that this new location would be acceptable. Today Rake, Wedge, and Lea live in a large area with a climbing tower and several other females.

Rake and Wedge, February 2003

SAMANTHA & CODY

SAMANTHA, a female tiger, and CODY, a male tiger, were mates who had lived together at the Pennsylvania facility that was shut down in 2000. They were separated by hundreds of miles when the USDA seized the owner's animals. Samantha was among the felines that were brought to EFRC by the USDA, but Cody ended up at another rescue center in Pennsylvania.

Two years later, when Samantha was moved into a large area at EFRC, it became possible for the Center to consider taking Cody. On October 30, 2002, workers from EFRC set out to get him, hoping that he and Samantha would remember each other. Cody seemed reluctant to get into the travel cage (felines almost always are), but after some encouragement he finally loaded. When he was unloaded the next morning and the travel cage was moved next to Samantha's enclosure, it soon became obvious that they knew each other. Their behavior was so friendly that it was decided to put Cody in with Samantha right away. Minutes later, they were happily reacquainted—all smiles and chuffs.

Cody is the father of two of the Munchkins—Isabella and Rolo. Samantha is the mother of two of the Munchkins—Sabrina and Tabitha.

Samantha, April 2002

Cody with Munchkins in the background, November 2002

Sierra & Montana, Goldie & Tish, Cuddles & Jody

Sierra, September 2001 (above)

Sierra and Montana, September 2001 (facing page)

THE ANIMALS that were rescued from Pennsylvania now live happily at EFRC. Sierra and Montana, a female and a male tiger, appear to have recovered nicely from the abuse they suffered at their former home. Tour guides seem to pass them by, but they can be quite entertaining for anyone with the time to observe them.

Tish and Goldie are two of the felines that came on the USDA truck. Like most lions, they tend to ignore people unless there is food to defend.

Cuddles and Jody, two female tigers, now live with Casey, a male tiger, and Nyla, a female tiger. They enjoy a large enclosure with a much-used climbing tower.

Goldie and Tish, July 2002

Goldie and Tish, June 2004

Cuddles and Jody with Casey and Nyla, July 2002

THE SOUTHERN BELLES

THE SOUTHERN BELLES are seven female lions who were part of a group of close to eighty felines that were found in Mississippi packed into tiny cages filled with feces and rotten bones. Many of the cats had festering sores on their skin. The Belles arrived at EFRC in 1997 after being featured on *Dateline NBC*. In July 1998, they got a 20,000-square-foot living area with a three-tier climbing tower. They quickly found the top. They can frequently be seen destroying one of their "indestructible" play balls. They are sometimes affectionately known as the "cafeteria line" at feeding time.

The Southern Belles, June 2003 (right)

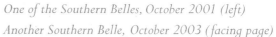

One of the Southern Belles, October 2001 (left)
Another Southern Belle, October 2003 (facing page)

TIGGER

TIGGER, a 500-pound male tiger, came to EFRC from a private facility in Ohio after attacking a worker who had mistakenly entered his cage. The worker, who recovered, was hospitalized with serious neck injuries. There was immediate pressure for the tiger to be destroyed, but other members of the community implored his owner to find a new home for him. When the staff of EFRC learned about the situation, they contacted the owner and offered to take Tigger.

EFRC workers traveled to Ohio to pick up Tigger, then took him directly to the University of Illinois Veterinary School for a complete checkup. After arriving at EFRC, he was quarantined for thirty days while his permanent home was being constructed. In late April 2001 he was given a clean bill of health and moved into his wooded habitat with a climbing tower and swimming tank.

Tigger is extremely friendly and loves to play a stalking game. Unfortunately, because of his location, he is not on the standard EFRC tour.

TIKA

TIKA is a female bobcat. Her former owners, who lived on a farm in northern Indiana, researched bobcats for two years before deciding to purchase one. When they felt they knew all they needed to know, they paid several hundred dollars for a twelve-week-old kitten from a breeder in Wisconsin. They had her spayed and declawed and kept her in their house as a pet.

Soon thereafter, health problems forced them to move into a house in town. Apparently their research had not revealed that all big felines spray and mark their territory. Their new home was Tika's new territory, and when the house began to reek of bobcat urine, the husband demanded that a new home be found for Tika, too.

Tika was eighteen months old when she was sent to the Hardy Lake Wildlife Rehabilitation Center. They agreed to take her on a trial basis and see if they could calm her down enough to use her for programming. Tika proved to be more than they bargained for, however; she was not trainable for the program. It had been agreed that if she did not work out, she would be transferred to EFRC. And so she was.

Although Tika was born and raised in captivity, you can see and feel the wildness in her eyes and in every move she makes. EFRC lets Tika be Tika. She loves playing with water coming out of a hose, and the staff enjoys her despite her prickly personality. She is quite large for a female bobcat.

Tika lives behind the shed near the EFRC entrance. Because she is stressed so easily, she is not on the tour.

Tika, July 2002 (left and right)

Tika, June 2004

Tika, August 2003

Visiting **EFRC**

First-time visitors should consider
contacting EFRC at:

Exotic Feline Rescue Center
2221 E. Ashboro Road
Center Point, IN 47840
812-835-1130
e-mail: efrc@claynet.com

For more information, visit the
Center's website:

http://www.exoticfelinerescuecenter.org

Office, motel, operating room, July 2004

Clyde, September 2003

STEPHEN D. McCLOUD has been a passionate
photographer since his teen years. His interests
include sports photography, natural landscapes,
oddities, and exotic felines. He has lived in
Terre Haute, Indiana, his entire life.

Photo by Stephanie Samaris

SPONSORING EDITOR
Linda Oblack

BOOK AND COVER DESIGNER
Pamela Rude

EDITORS
Jane Lyle and Miki Bird

TYPEFACES
Perpetua and Univers

PRINTER
Four Colour Imports

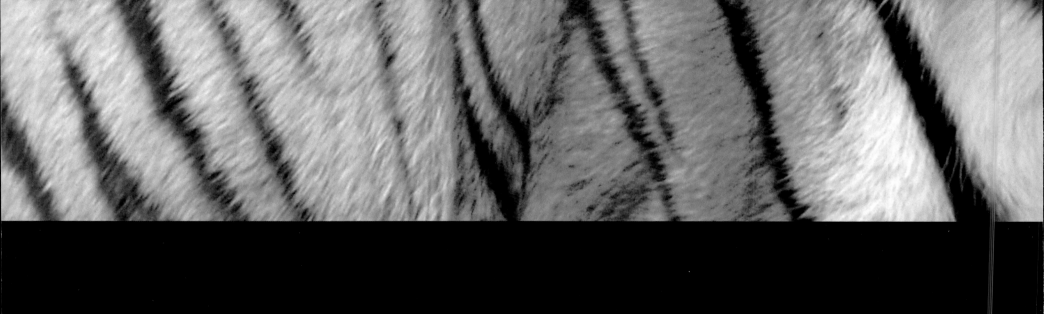